SEP 1 9 2012

P9-CLI-260

Let's Play Dress Up
I WANT TO BE A PRINCESS

Rebekah Joy Shirley
Photography by Chris Fairclough

WINDMILL
BOOKS

New York

Published in 2012 by Windmill Books, An Imprint of Rosen Publishing
29 East 21st Street, New York, NY 10010

Copyright © 2012 Arcturus Publishing Limited

All rights reserved. No part of this book may be reproduced in any form
without permission in writing from the publisher, except by a reviewer.

Series concept: Discovery Books Ltd, 2 College Street, Ludlow, Shropshire SY8 1AN, UK
www.discoverybooks.net

Managing editor: Laura Durman
Editor: Rebecca Hunter
Designer: Blink Media
Photography: Chris Fairclough

Library of Congress Cataloging-in-Publication Data

Shirley, Rebekah Joy.
 I want to be a princess / by Rebekah Joy Shirley. — 1st ed.
    p. cm. — (Let's play dress up)
Includes index.
ISBN 978-1-61533-356-1 (library binding) — ISBN 978-1-61533-394-3 (pbk.) — ISBN 978-1-61533-459-9 (6-pack)
1. Handicraft—Juvenile literature. 2. Children's costumes—Juvenile literature. 3. Princesses—Juvenile literature. I. Title.
TT171.S55 2012
646.4'78—dc22

2010050407

The author and photographer would like to acknowledge the following for their help in preparing this book:
the staff and pupils of Chad Vale Primary School, Iqrah Choudhury, Jack Coady, Rosie Palmer-Downes,
Abbie Sangha, Sharnai Walker, Annia J Wright.

Printed in China

CPSIA Compliance Information: Batch #AS2011WM: For Further Information contact Windmill Books, New York, New York at 1-866-478-0556
SL001743US

CONTENTS

Some of the projects in this book require the use of needles, pins, and safety pins.
We would advise that young children are supervised by a responsible adult.

A GORGEOUS GOWN

Making a costume can be messy work! Make sure you cover all surfaces with newspaper before you start.

One of the best things about being a princess is having lots of lovely dresses. This gorgeous ball **gown** is for wearing on very special **occasions**.

To make your own gown you will need:
- A T-shirt
- A ruler
- A compass
- Sparkly net (3-ft. length)
- A pair of scissors
- A pen or pencil
- A needle
- Cotton thread
- Craft gems
- Craft glue and a paintbrush
- A strip of fabric to fit around your waist
- An old lace or net curtain
- White pantyhose or leggings

1 Measure the join between the body of the T-shirt and the sleeve, from shoulder to underarm. Double the length and set your compass to that size.

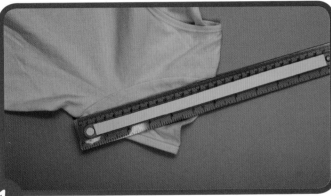

2 Use the compass to draw a semicircle onto the sparkly net. Cut the semicircle out. Then repeat so that you have two semicircles.

TIP:

If you cannot draw onto your material, draw the semicircle onto a piece of paper. Cut the semicircle out and pin it to the material. Then use it as a **template** to cut around.

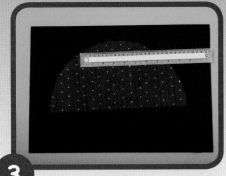

3 Measure the width of the T-shirt join (from step 1) straight across the curved edge of each semicircle and mark.

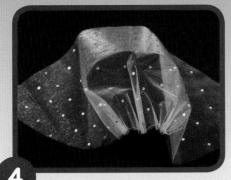

4 Sew around the curved edge between the two marks you have made. Try to make all of your stitches the same length. Then pull the cotton so that the material pleats and tie a knot.

To make your princess dress even more special, loop the rest of your sparkly net over the top of your skirt!

5 Sew the bottom corners of each semicircle to the T-shirt where the underarm joins the body. Then sew over the pleats to join the pleated section to the shoulder of the T-shirt.

6 Glue craft gems around the neck of the T-shirt.

7 Tie a strip of fabric around your waist. Loop the lace or net curtain over the fabric strip to make a skirt.

A STUNNING SASH

A stunning sash will make a princess's ball gown look even more special. You could make several sashes in different colors to wear on different occasions.

Make a sash using:
A strip of colored material measuring about 3 ft.
A craft knife
A piece of cardboard
A ruler
Gold paint and a paintbrush
A pen or pencil

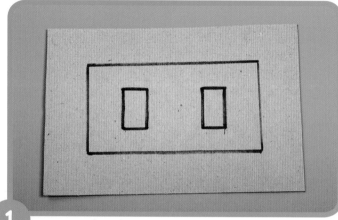

1 With a ruler draw a rectangle about 3 in. x 6 in. on cardboard. Draw two smaller rectangles inside the large one.

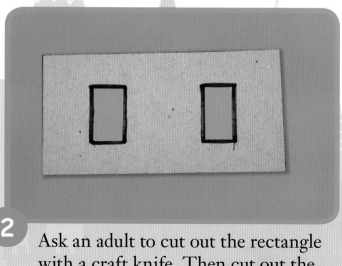

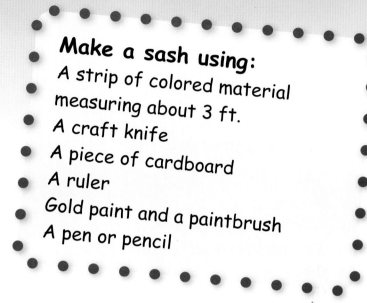

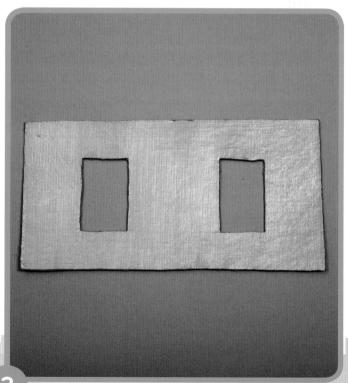

2 Ask an adult to cut out the rectangle with a craft knife. Then cut out the smaller rectangles to make a **buckle**.

3 Paint your buckle gold. You could also glue on some craft gems if you like.

4 Thread the material strip through the buckle so the gold side is showing and in the middle.

Tie the material around your waist in a bow at the back or at the side. The sash will hold your dress together and make it look beautiful!

DAINTY TOES

As a princess you will be invited to dance at lots of balls. Like Cinderella, you will want to wear pretty slippers—but perhaps not made of glass!

To make your slippers you will need:
A pair of ballet shoes
Ribbon
Craft glue and a paintbrush
Shiny beads
Craft gems
A needle

TIP:
If your shoes are hard to sew through, ask an adult to make holes in them. Then you can thread the ribbon through the holes.

1 Glue the gems or beads onto your shoes using craft glue.

2 Carefully sew ribbon along the edges of the opening in a crisscross pattern.

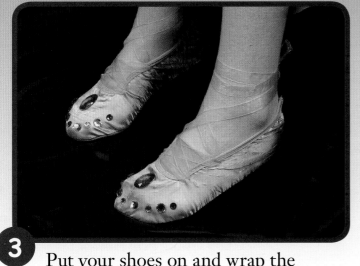

3 Put your shoes on and wrap the ribbons around your legs. Then tie them in a bow.

You will be able to dance all night in these beautiful slippers.

GLAMOROUS GLOVES

Princesses like to be very fashionable. To be a really stylish princess you will need a pair of long, elegant gloves.

You can make your own gloves using:
A pair of footless pantyhose
A pair of scissors
Two craft gems
Craft glue and a paintbrush
Thin, colored ribbon
A needle
Thin elastic

1 Cut off the pantyhose legs.

TIP: If you do not have footless pantyhose, cut the feet off. Then turn the edge over and sew that too.

2 Turn over the top edge of each leg and sew big stitches of elastic around it. Pull tight and tie the elastic in a bow.

3 Glue a gem in the middle at one end of each glove.

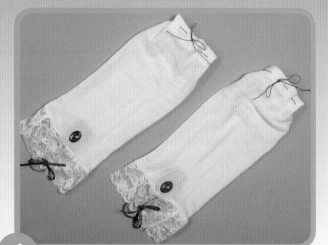

4 Sew a loop of ribbon at the end of each glove above the gem. Knot the ribbon and tie it in a bow. When you put the glove on the ribbon loop will go over your middle finger.

Your prince will not be able to resist taking your hand for a dance if you are wearing these gloves!

A COURTLY CLOAK

During the winter months a princess must keep warm. A cloak is like a coat or a blanket that can be worn over your fine clothes.

Make your own cloak using:
An old curtain, bed sheet or length of material
Colored ribbon
A needle
A pair of scissors
A ruler

1 Cut the material into a rectangle about 3 ft. x 5 ft. Sew a piece of ribbon along one of the shorter edges of the rectangle.

2 Mark a point about 16 in. in from the center of the ribbon. Sew some more ribbon from the edges to this point in a V-shape.

3 Pull the ribbon slightly and then knot either side. This will make the hood of your cloak.

4 Use the ribbon to loosely tie the cloak around your neck.

When you leave the ball at midnight your cloak will keep you warm and cozy!

TO CROWN IT ALL

A princess has a beautiful crown to wear on her head. This crown is called a tiara.

To make your own tiara you will need:
Cardboard
A pen or pencil
A pair of scissors
Craft glue and a paintbrush
A ruler
Sequins
A craft knife
Craft gems
A hole punch
Two pieces of ribbon
Silver paint and a paintbrush

1 On cardboard draw an outline of the tiara and cut it out. The tiara should be about 10 in. long.

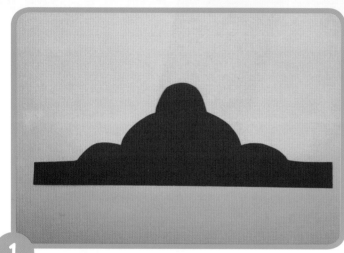

2 Draw **symmetrical** shapes on the cardboard. Ask an adult to cut them out with a craft knife.

3 Paint the tiara silver.

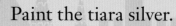

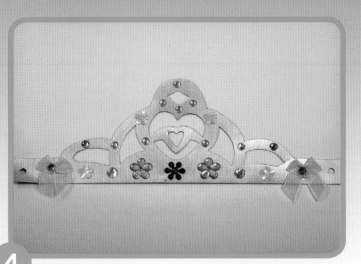

Use the ribbons to tie the tiara around your head. Now go and dazzle your **courtiers** in this lovely tiara!

4 Punch a hole in the cardboard at each end of your tiara. The hole should be about ½ in. from the edge. Then glue sequins and gems to your tiara.

5 Thread a ribbon through each hole and knot.

Simsbury Public Library
Children's Room

ALL THAT GLITTERS

Princesses have lots of jewelry. The bigger and sparklier the better!

1 Pour the glue, paint, sequins, and glitter into separate plastic trays. Then roll the pasta in the trays.

Make your jewellery using:

Uncooked pasta tubes
Paint
Sequins
Glitter
Craft glue
4 plastic trays
A 5-ft. length of ribbon
An old pair of clip-on earrings
A ruler

TIP:

If you want your pasta pieces to look different, roll some of them in the paint only, some of them in the paint and glitter trays, and some of them in the glue and sequin trays.

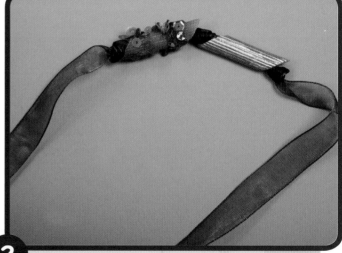

2 Cut a 24-in. and a 16-in. length of ribbon. When the pasta has dried, thread the pieces onto the ribbons. Tie knots between the pieces of pasta.

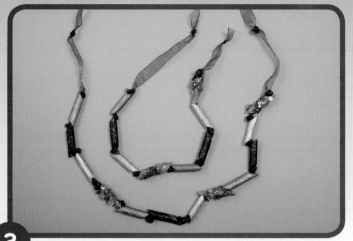

3 Continue adding pieces of pasta and tying knots in-between until you have 2 in. of ribbon left at each end. Use this to tie up your bracelet and necklace.

4 To make the earrings, cut the remaining ribbon in half. Knot the end of the ribbon and thread two pieces of pasta onto it, with a knot between them. Tie the top of the ribbon onto a clip-on earring.

Dressed up in all your jewelry, you will truly sparkle at the ball!

A BEJEWELED BROOCH

A brooch is like a badge covered with lots of jewels. This beautiful brooch is the finishing touch to a princess's jewelry.

Make a princess brooch using:
- Cardboard
- A ruler
- Silver paint and a paintbrush
- A pair of scissors
- Sequins
- A safety pin
- Craft gems
- Scotch tape
- Craft glue and a paintbrush
- Glitter
- A pen or pencil

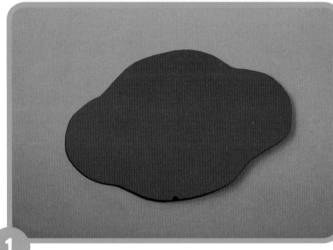

1 Draw the shape of your brooch onto cardboard and cut it out. The brooch should be about 4 in. long.

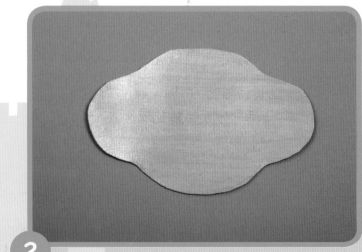

2 Paint the brooch silver.

3 Decorate your brooch with sequins, gems, and glitter.

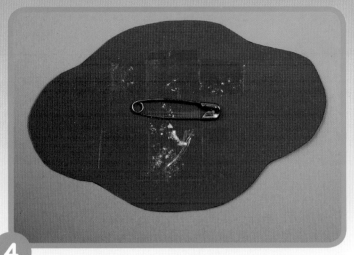

4 Stick a safety pin to the back of your brooch using Scotch tape.

Wearing this brooch will show everyone what a **wealthy** and **charming** princess you are!

TIP:
Use the brooch you have made to fasten your cloak.

A HEAVENLY HAT

Princesses do not wear their tiaras all the time. When they go traveling or out to watch **tournaments** they need a suitable hat.

To make a hat you will need:
Colored cardboard
A pair of scissors
Ribbon or strips of fabric
Craft glue and a paintbrush
Colored paint and a paintbrush
A marker pen
Sequins
A ruler
Elastic
A hole punch

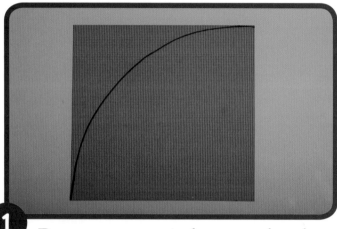

1 Draw a quarter circle onto colored cardboard. The straight sides should be about 10 in. long.

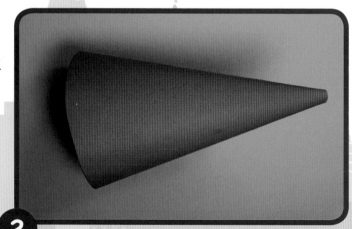

2 Cut out the quarter circle and glue it together to make a cone shape. Cut the top off the cone to make a hole.

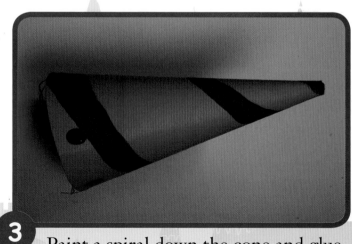

3 Paint a spiral down the cone and glue sequins at the bottom.

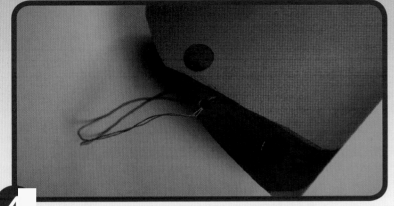

4 Punch a hole at the bottom of the hat on either side. Thread a piece of elastic through the holes. The elastic will go under your chin to hold your hat on.

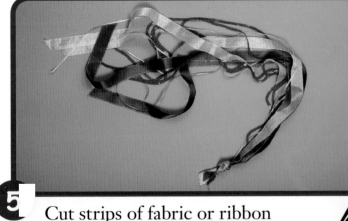

5 Cut strips of fabric or ribbon about 30 in. long. Knot them together at one end.

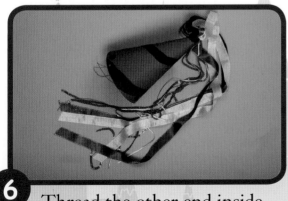

6 Thread the other end inside the hat through the hole in the top. The knot should hold the strips in place.

This hat will make you look like a truly magical princess!

ALONG CAME A PRINCE...

Every princess needs a prince to take her to the ball.

A prince would wear a stylish vest to the ball. Make your own using:

- A blue pillowcase
- Colored tape
- A marker pen
- A pair of scissors

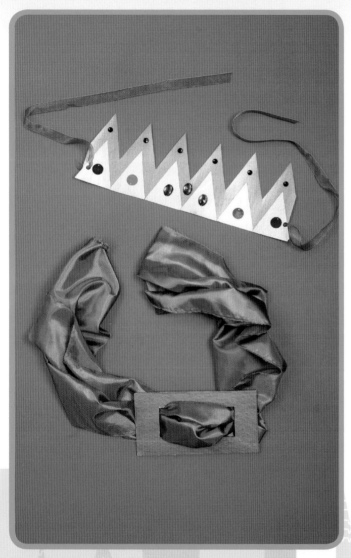

Use the instructions for the princess sash and tiara to make a prince's belt and crown. You might choose to paint the prince's crown gold and use gold or blue material for the belt.

1 Fold the pillowcase in half. Cut a quarter circle in the top corner that is not folded to make the armholes.

2 Unfold the pillowcase. Draw a line up the center and a V-shape at the top for the neckline.

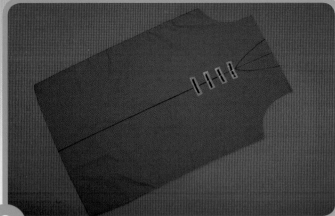

3 Stick pieces of colored tape in **horizontal** lines across the centre. Draw thick, black lines across the middle of the tape with a marker pen.

4 Cut along the lines through the front piece of the pillowcase. Do not cut through both layers. Cut the waistcoat to length and round off the corners.

Now your prince is ready to go out and create a **sensation** at the ball!

GLOSSARY

buckle (BUH-kul) the fastening on the end of a belt
charming (CHAHRM-ing) attractive and pleasant
courtier (KOR-tee-ur) somebody who spends time at a royal court
gown (GOWN) a special dress often worn to balls
horizontal (hor-ih-ZON-til) in a flat line from left to right
occasion (uh-KAY-zhun) an important event
sensation (sen-SAY-shun) something that creates lots of public interest
symmetrical (sih-MEH-trih-kul) being exactly the same on both sides
template (TEM-plut) a shape cut out to reproduce a pattern or shape
tournament (TOR-nuh-ment) a sports event made up of games or contests
wealthy (WEL-thee) very rich

FURTHER INFORMATION

Clibbon, Meg. *My World of Sparkly Princesses. Midwest City, OK:* Zero to Ten, 2010.
LaVigna Coyle, Carmela. *Do Princesses Really Kiss Frogs?* Flagstaff, AZ: Rising Moon, 2005.
Lechermeier, Philippe. *The Secret Lives of Princesses.* New York, NY: Sterling, 2010.

WEB SITES

For Web resources related to the subject of this book, go to: www.windmillbooks.com/weblinks and select this book's title.

INDEX

Simsbury Public Library
Children's Book
725 Hopmeadow Street
Simsbury, CT 06070